Official Mac OS X Guidebook

AMARPREET SINGH

THE THOUGHT FLAME
TURNING SPARK INTO FLAME

info@thethoughtflame.com

www.thethoughtflame.com

Table of Contents

Introduction

This book contains proven steps and strategies on how to use Mac OS X Yosemite to its Fullest Potential.

When an OS X is released, it comes packed with hundreds of new features, upgrades, enhancements, and improvements. However, not all of these features and upgrades are advertised or promoted, and, therefore, we only know about the major upgrades that are advertised by Apple.

In this guide you can learn about the major as well as minor upgrades and new features that come with OS X Yosemite. You can also learn how to setup your Macs, iPads, and iPod Touch to receive calls and messages directly from your cellular network, or how to set up and use the Hand off and Continuity features on Yosemite. There are several tips and tricks included at the

1

end of the book, including how to use the annotation features.

Thanks again for downloading this book, I hope you enjoy it!

Chapter 1 – OS X Yosemite

OS X Yosemite is Apple's eleventh major release for the Mac computers, both iMacs and MacBooks. It was announced at WWDC 2014 on 2nd June 2014, and is the first software in over a decade that Apple released to the public for testing. OS X Yosemite beta was free to download to for the first one million users. The first beta was made available for download on 24th July 2014. Apple subsequently released several more beta versions until finally releasing OS X Yosemite to public on 26th October 2014. It is named after the Yosemite National Park in California. Yosemite is free to download on all compatible devices.

Apple has completely redesigned the software and given it a new and fresh look, keeping up with the scheme of iOS 7 for iPhones and iPads. It comes packed with powerful new features and connects iDevices like iPhones and iPads much more than ever before. It can be downloaded for free from the App Store on iMacs and MacBooks.

Design & Interface

Yosemite brings a new design and interface to the Mac and keeps up with the same colour and design scheme that was introduced to iDevices with iOS 7 upgrade. The windows and toolbars are now translucent, and the icons, fonts, buttons, etc. have been redesigned as well. Everything has been given a fresh and new look. The design is aesthetically pleasing and makes full use of the retina display, enhancing the overall beauty of the interface. The translucent sidebars also give you a glimpse of whatever is behind the active window. Toolbars for all major applications, as well as minor ones, have been streamlined. This makes them take a very little space, leaving more space for the windows on the screen, increasing the work or viewing area, and making overall use more efficient; it is especially useful for MacBooks with smaller screens. The colour scheme of stoplights is now followed by the buttons, with red, yellow, and green buttons at the corner of the screen now working as close, minimise, and full; the extra button for full screen has been removed.

Moreover, the place that is mostly used for launching apps, the Dock, has gotten a makeover too. The doc also has a translucent and a flatter look now, with the icons for applications redesigned to make them easy to identify. It comes with new fonts and typeface for the menu bars, app windows, etc. to make reading more consistent and legible.

Notification Center

The notification centre has also been made more powerful. It has a new Today view that allows you to quickly see whatever you want. A new shortcuts lets you swipe at the edge of your track pad with two fingers to quickly open up the notification center. You can see a brief summary of the upcoming events for the day, as well as reminders and birthdays. You can add widgets as well, like weather, calendar, time, stock prices, calculator, etc., or you can download new widgets from the App Store if you want.

Spotlight

One of the most used applications on a Mac, the Spotlight, has also been redesigned and advanced. As Apple says, it is the fastest way to find things on a Mac. Now it has gotten even better; not only has it been redesigned but a lot more features have been added to it as well. While searching, you now get a comprehensive preview so you can find exactly what you are looking for and view it in detail before opening it. It also gets information from Wikipedia, news websites, iTunes, Maps, movie listings, etc. The spotlight now appears at the centre of the screen, instead of the corner, and the previews are interactive so you can view documents, send emails, and even make calls with a single click. It includes documents, photos, content from the iTunes store, currency conversion, news, contacts, and more.

iOS Connectivity

One of the best features that OS X Yosemite introduces and that set it apart from any of the previous OS X releases is the power it brings by combining and unifying Macs and MacBooks with iPhones and iPads. You can receive your phone calls, make calls, and send and receive messages on your Macs and MacBooks. With Handoff you can start doing something on one device and continue it on another. Moreover, your Macs and MacBooks can connect to the Internet so easily that you will not even have to take your phone out of your pocket. You can also share files between your Macs and iDevices with AirDrop.

Empowered Apps

All the apps have been empowered so you can do things more easily and efficiently. Safari now makes use of energy saving technologies to save the battery and has a tab view as well so you can easily switch between different websites. Your favourite pages are not limited to the respective devices only but are synced and available on all of your iDevices. Compared to other browsers, the advanced energy saving mechanism now gives you 2-3 hours more battery when surfing the Internet on Safari. Mail now lets you annotate images and PDFs, send large files, and add signatures to your emails without having to leave the application at all. Combined with iCloud, you can send files up to 5GB in mail. The Messages app now lets you have group conversations on your Macs and MacBooks, add titles to messages, share conversations, and even send audio messages. And Family Sharing allows you to share content with up to 6 members of your family. You can not only share stuff but your family can also make purchases without needing your credit card info at all. For members under 18 years of age, you have the option to approve any purchases they make before anything is actually bought, though this option is not available for family members over 18 years of age.

The Apple devices have become more connected and powerful than ever before.

Chapter 2 – Enabling Cellular Network Calls and Text Message Forwarding on your Mac/MacBook

Apple's OS X Yosemite can transform the way you do things on your Macs, MacBooks, iPhones, and iPads, but first you will have to learn how to use all those new features.

Cellular Network Calls on your Macs

Let's see how to setup your iDevices so you can make and receive cellular network calls from them. There are a few requirements for this which are as follows:

All devices need to be connected to the same WiFi network

All devices should be running iOS 8.1 or above (Macs and MacBooks should be running OS X Yosemite)

All devices should be using the same iCloud account

Note: If there are multiple iPhones in the same house and all are connected to the same iCloud account then this can cause problems because any call received on any phone will ring on all devices and can be answered by anyone. It can be prevented by making sure that only one iPhone has the iCloud ID you want to answer calls with associated with it.

Setting Up on your Mac or MacBook

First you will have to enable your computer to make and receive calls, and to do that you will need to:

Open FaceTime on your Mac or MacBook

Go to 'Preferences'

Check the box that says 'iPhone Cellular Calls'

You will also have the option to choose which number or email you want the receiver to see when you make a call. It can be selected from the 'Start new calls from:' dropdown menu; anyone who does not have you in his or her contacts will see the number/email you choose here. If you ever want to disable this service, you can simply go to FaceTime preferences and uncheck the 'iPhone Cellular Calls' option.

Setting Up on your iDevices

Next you need to enable the same thing on your iPhone and iPad(s). Following are the steps for setting that up:

Go to settings on your device

Go to FaceTime in settings

Turn on the 'iPhone Cellular Calls' option

The phone will ring on all the devices that have this option turned on. If you have an iPad, a MacBook, and an iPhone, and would like to receive calls only on your iPhone and MacBook, then you only need to enable these options on those devices only. You have full control over which devices will receive the call and which devices will not.

To make cellular calls from your MacBook or iPad you have two options. You can either make calls directly through the FaceTime app, or you can open up Contacts and make calls from there. You will be able to choose whether you want to make a FaceTime video, audio, or a cellular network call. You can also make calls to listed numbers directly from Safari.

Receiving a Call

Now if someone calls you using FaceTime or cellular network, all the devices that are allowed to receive the call will ring. Your iPhone, iPad, and Mac or MacBook will ring at the same time, and you will be able to see the caller's name and numbers; you will also be able to see the caller's picture if it is in your contacts and you have added a picture for it.

The notification for calls appears on Macs and MacBooks on the upper right hand corner of the screen. You can either 'Accept' the call or 'Decline' it. All the options will be available, including a little arrow that allows you to send a quick message to let the caller know why you can't answer; you can set a reminder for the call from there as well. If you 'Accept' the call on your Mac or MacBook, you will be able to talk directly. The built in mic and speakers will be used, unless you have headphones plugged in.

If you ignore the call or miss it, there will be a notification for it in the notification centre for you to check later. The process of receiving calls on an iPad is completely the same as receiving them on iPhone.

If you are on call on your iPad or Mac/MacBook and need to leave the house or office but still want to continue the call, you can do that too. Simply turn your iPhone on, and you will see a green bar on the top of your iPhone's screen that will say, 'Touch to return to call'. Click on it and the call will be transferred to your phone instantly.

Setting Up Messages

Keeping up with the Continuity features of Yosemite is the Text Message Forwarding. When enabled, it allows you to send and receive cellular network messages directly from your iDevices. iOS 8.1 is required for this feature. Previously, only iMessages were synced across all devices while the cellular network messages were limited to your phones. If you enable Text Message Forwarding, you can message anyone who is not using iMessages, directly from your iPod, iPad, or MacBook, etc.

Following are the requirements for setting up SMS Relay:

All devices need to be connected to the same WiFi network

All devices should be running iOS 8.1 or above

All devices should be using the same iCloud account

Note: Just like for cellular network calls, if different iPhones are using the same iCloud account then Messages will become confusing, so make sure that only one iPhone is connected to the iCloud account.

Setting UP Text Message Forwarding

Following are the steps for setting up Text Message Forwarding:

Turn on your iDevice (iPad, iPod Touch, etc.)

Go to the 'Settings'

Go to the 'Messages' in 'Settings'

Click on 'Send & Receive' and make sure that you are signed in with the iCloud ID you want to use

Return to your Mac/MacBook

Open the 'Messages' app and go to 'Preferences'

Check whether or not you are signed in with your iCloud account

If you are not signed in, sign in

Once you sign in, the iCloud account will appear in the 'Accounts' tab in 'Preferences'

Then you will have to set this up on your iPhone. Here's how to do that:

Go to 'Settings'

Then scroll down and open the 'Messages' in 'Settings'

Click on 'Text Message Forwarding'

Then turn it on for the devices that you want your messages to be relayed to

You will see your iCloud devices listed there

If your MacBook and iPhone are using the same iCloud account, you can enable it from for your MacBook from there

When you turn it on for a device from there, a prompt will appear on your phone and a pop-up on the selected device

The pop-up on the device will have a confirmation code that you will have to type in the prompt on your iPhone

Once you have competed all the steps mentioned above, your Text Message Forwarding will be set up, and you will be able to send and receive messages using the selected device(s). If you want to send a message using your cellular network through the Messages app on Mac/MacBook, you will have to manually select the contact's number as the Messages app is set to send iMessages by default.

Chapter 3 – Setting up Handoff on Yosemite

This one is especially useful for people who work using iPads, iPhones, or Macs and constantly need to update the data on all devices. When Handoff is enabled, you can start a task on one device and continue it on another. For instance, if you are writing an email on your Mac then you can stop anytime and continue it on your iPhone, or if you are reading an email on your iPad, you can stop anywhere and pick right up on your MacBook, or if you are writing an article in the Notes app on your Mac, you can stop anywhere and continue from the very point you left it at on your iPad. The Handoff works seamlessly on all devices. A separate dock on your Mac/MacBook will indicate what Handoff compatible app is running on your iOS device, and on your iOS device there will be an icon to indicate that the app is being used on the Mac or MacBook or another iOS device. Following applications are compatible with Handoff:

Calendar

Contacts

Keynote

Mail

Map

Messages

Note

Number

Pages

Reminder

Safari

Apple has also allowed the developers to make use of Handoff features so many more compatible applications will appear soon.

Handoff works on the late 2013 Mac Pro, MacBook Pro, MacBook Air, and the 2012 iMac as well as on the latest one. The iOS devices also need to be running iOS 8 and should have Bluetooth turned on for Handoff to work. All your devices, OS X and iOS, should be connected to the same iCloud account.

Enabling Handoff

To enable Handoff on an iOS device, here's what you need to do:

First, go to settings on the iOS device

Then go to 'General' in settings

Click on 'Handoff & Suggested Apps'

From there, turn on 'Handoff'

Next, you need to enable Handoff on your Mac or MacBook. Following are the steps for enabling Handoff on your Mac/MacBook:

Turn on your Mac/MacBook

Go to System Preferences

Click on the 'General' icon

Scroll down and check the box next to 'Allow Handoff between this Mac and your iCloud devices'

Once that is done, Handoff will be set up and ready to go.

Using Handoff

Now, we will go through an example to give you a better understanding of using Handoff. For our example we will use the Notes app on an iPad and a Mac and make use of the Handoff.

You can open up the Notes app on your iPad to start writing something, say a blog post. With Handoff enabled, when you are writing in Notes on your iPad, a Notes icon will appear in a separate dock on your Mac. This icon will also have an iPad icon on the upper right corner of it; this is to tell you which iOS device is using the said app. You can also see this in the App Switcher by pressing and holding the 'command' and 'tab' buttons at the same time on your keyboard. Now, click on that Notes icon in the new dock to open it up and continue working on it. When you click on it, the app will open up and take you right where you stopped writing your blog post on the iPad.

Chapter 4 – Setting up Instant Hotspot

If your iPhone is running iOS 8.1 then it can be used as an Instant Hotspot for your Mac, MacBook, iPad, iPod Touch, etc. All devices need to be running latest firmwares. This is particularly useful when you do not have access to WiFi on any of your devices, but have cellular data network available on your phone. There is no need to set up the Personal Hotspot like before. When the devices are close by, the phone's personal hotspot will automatically appear in their WiFi lists and all you will have to do is select it. The Internet will turn off to save battery life when none of the devices are using it. Sometimes personal hotspot option does not appear, and to prevent that from happening, make sure that you have entered the Internet settings. Here's how to enter the

Internet settings:

Go to 'Settings' on your iPhone

Click on 'Cellular'

Click on 'Cellular Data Network'

Then enter the settings for 'Personal Hotspot,' 'Cellular Data Network,' and 'LTE'

When your iPhone is connected to the Internet and other devices are connected to it through Instant Hotspot or Personal Hotspot, the top of your iPhone screen will turn blue and will show the tether sign. If more than one device is using your personal hotspot, the number of devices in use will appear around the tether sign. The name of the Personal Hotspot connection will also flash on the blue bar on the top of your iPhone's screen.

Chapter 5 – OS X Yosemite Tips and Tricks

Spotlight on Top

To keep Spotlight on top of all other windows to easily search for what you need to, open up Spotlight and then right click on the Spotlight icon (magnifying glass) on the top right corner of the screen. The icon will turn blue to indicate that Spotlight will stay on top of all windows. Left click it to return to the normal mode.

Quickly Disconnect from a Network Connection

In the previous versions of OS X, you had to open up the network preferences to disconnect from the WiFi you were connected to. This has been simplified in OS X Yosemite. To disconnect from a network quickly, hold the 'alt' key and click on the Wifi sign on the menu bar. The option to disconnect will appear in the dropdown menu below the name of the WiFi you are connected to.

View iCloud Storage in Detail

To view the iCloud storage in details, simply open up iCloud on Yosemite and look at the bottom of the screen. The storage will be categorised in the same way as it is shown for iPhone, iPad, and iPod on iTunes.

Importing Bookmarks from Other Web Browsers

In Yosemite you can easily import your bookmarks from Google Chrome and Mozilla

Firefox to Safari. To do that, here's what you need to do:

Open up Safari

Click on File

Click on 'Import From'

Then select the browser you want to import bookmarks from

Done!

Pink and Brown Highlights

There is a minor new thing introduced in Yosemite that some people (fans of brown or pink colour) will love. Now you can go to Setting, General, and in Highlight colour you will be able to choose Pink or Brown colour from the dropdown menu.

Annotating

The Preview app also has a lot of annotation tools now. Open up a photo or PDF in the Preview app and then click on the tool box icon at the top right of the screen, and it will open up a number of new tools. These tools include:

A pen icon for sketching, which allows you to draw rough shapes and then automatically changes them to proper shapes, kind of like sketching autocorrection. You can draw a rough triangle and it will automatically be corrected to a perfect triangle. You will also have the option to change your drawing back to its original rough shape.

You can also add new shapes to whatever you have open in the Preview app. When you click on the shapes icon, you will get a drop down menu that will let you choose from different shapes. You can drag a shape on to your photo/documents and then adjust its size.

Other new features include Shaded Mask and Loupe.

Automatic Update Installation

Unlike previous versions of OS X, Yosemite has the option to automatically install app, OS X, as well as data files and security updates. You can opt for this in System Preferences in the App Store settings. Check the boxes next to all the things that you want to set for automatic updates.

Update Feeds of Websites

Yosemite has also brought an old OS X feature back: the ability to tune into RSS feeds of different websites. Simply click on the RSS/Atom link on a web page to add it to your collection.

Changing FaceTime Ring Tone

Yes, you heard that right. You can change the ringtone for FaceTime. Here's how to do it:

Open up the FaceTime app

Go to its 'Preferences'

Then scroll down to where it says 'Ringtone' and select the ringtone you want.

You can also change the alert sound for messages. To do that, here's what you need to do:

Open up the Messages app

Go to its 'Preferences'

Go to the 'General' tab

Select the tone you want from the 'Message Received Sound' dropdown menu.

Quickly Viewing all Attachments Sent

In Yosemite, you now have the option to view all the attachments you have sent in a conversation in Messages. Simply open up the conversation and then click on details to quickly get a peek at everything you have sent. This feature is also available in iOS 8 for Messages for iPhones, iPads, and iPod Touch.

Quickly Closing a Tab in Safari

For this you will require a PC mouse with a wheel. To quickly kill the tab that is open on your screen, hover your mouse over it and then press the wheel. The tab will be instantly closed, but can be brought back by pressing Command and Z at the same time.

Signatures

You can also sign documents using your track pad. Open up a document in Preview, then click on the tool box, and then click on the signature icon. A new window will pop up for you to enter your signature in. It will have two options, select the one for the track pad and then create your own signature using your finger.

Duck Duck Go

Apple has proved that is actually cares for its consumers' privacy. It has now introduced Duck Duck Go as a search engine in Yosemite, as well as in iOS. Duck Duck Go is a search engine that does not store your data or track your information, unlike other search engines.

To change your default search engine to Duck Duck Go, here's what you need to do:

Open up Safari

Go to 'Preferences'

Then go to the 'Search' tab

Then select 'DuckDuckGo' from the 'Search Engine' dropdown menu.

OS X Yosemite is packed with many more features that you can look up on the Internet or explore yourself. Not all the features are advertised by Apple as it only promotes the most significant and major features, but the smaller upgrades and features are very helpful too.

If you haven't downloaded and installed OS X Yosemite yet, you can get it for free from the Mac App Store; it can be found in the 'Featured' tab.

<u>Conclusion</u>

Thank you again for downloading this book!

I hope this book was able to help you to use OS X Yosemite to its fullest potential.

The next step is to use iOS 8 to its fullest potential.

About Us

The Thought Flame is committed to add value to its customers through various books, online courses and other resources. You can learn more about us and our books at www.thethoughtflame.com.

Don't forget to check out our amazing **online video courses** at www.thethoughtflame.com/courses/ to take your knowledge to another level.

To check out our **extraordinary collection of diet/cookbooks**, visit http://www.thethoughtflame.com/category/non-fictional/cookbooks/ .

As a part of our valued relationship with our customers, we keep providing you free promotional books, courses and other stuff on subscribing with us on our site. We have a strict anti-spam policy and assure you no spam mails will be sent to your mailbox.

To subscribe with us, visit

www.thethoughtflame.com.

Like our work and would like to say thanks?

Buy us a cup of coffee at

www.thethoughtflame.com/coffee/

<u>Author</u>

Amarpreet Singh is an avid learner and his passion for education has made him travel, work and study all across the world. He holds three masters degrees, including MBA, from top universities in Asia.

He is author of dozens of books, many of which are Amazon's bestseller, varying in various topics and categories. He also teaches many online courses having thousands of students across the world.

He has a keen interest in international affairs, economics, global poverty and politics, financial markets and entrepreneurship, and strives to be part of a community that shares the same passion.

He has worked as consultant with organizations like Airbus and The World Bank.

He loves travelling and learning about new cultures, and has been fortunate to live/work/travel/study in countries like India, China, Korea, US, South Africa, Japan, Philippines, Singapore, Canada etc., and learn about the culture and lifestyle in each of them.

To check out more of his work, visit www.thethoughtflame.com